ALTERNATOR
BOOKS™

WHO INVENTED THE
TELEPHONE?

BELL VS. MEUCCI

Susan E. Hamen

Lerner Publications ◆ Minneapolis

For my mom, who still refuses to
upgrade to a smartphone

Lerner Publications Company
A division of Lerner Publishing Group, Inc.
241 First Avenue North
Minneapolis, MN 55401 USA

For reading levels and more information, look up this title at www.lernerbooks.com.

Main body text set in Aptifer Slab Regular 11.5/18.
Typeface provided by Linotype AG.

Library of Congress Cataloging-in-Publication Data

Names: Hamen, Susan E., author.
Title: Who invented the telephone? : Bell vs. Meucci / by Susan E. Hamen.
Description: Minneapolis : Lerner Publications, [2018] | Series: STEM Smackdown |
    Audience: Grades 4 to 6. | Audience: Ages 8–12. | Includes bibliographical references
    and index.
Identifiers: LCCN 2017030079| ISBN 9781512483222 (lb) | ISBN 9781541512108 (pb) |
    ISBN 9781512483284 (eb pdf)
Subjects: LCSH: Telephone—History—Juvenile literature. | Bell, Alexander Graham,
    1847–1922—Juvenile literature. | Meucci, Antonio, 1808–1889—Juvenile literature.
Classification: LCC TK6165 .H36 2018 | DDC 621.386092/2—dc23

LC record available at https://lccn.loc.gov/2017030079

Manufactured in the United States of America
1-43335-33155-9/28/2017

CONTENTS

A SMARTER PHONE

You decide to throw a surprise birthday party for your friend. You ask your dad for help getting ready for the party. He takes out his smartphone, and you pick out some streamers and balloons. With a few taps on the phone, your dad orders the supplies to be delivered to your front door.

You and your dad open another window on the phone and check out some cupcake recipes. You pick one that looks good and turn on the music app so you can sing along as you make the cupcakes together. With the cupcakes finished and the decorations on their way, you call your friends and invite them to the party.

Smartphones give you access to many kinds of information right at your fingertips.

The first smartphone was released to the public in 1992, but people didn't start using the term *smartphone* until 1995.

Smartphones can do many different things. Besides making phone calls, users can get directions from a map app, enjoy a virtual reality experience using a special headset, and video chat with friends far away. As advanced as smartphones have become, their history began in the late nineteenth century with the invention of the telephone. Two men chased the dream of communicating instantly over long distances. Most Americans will say Alexander Graham Bell won the race. But anyone who knows about Antonio Santi Giuseppe Meucci, the other player in the telephone game, might have a different opinion about who deserves the prize.

CHAPTER 1

THE DEFENDING CHAMP

In 1871, twenty-four-year-old British-born Alexander Graham Bell moved to Boston, Massachusetts. There he became a speech professor at Boston University. In addition to teaching, he also studied the human voice.

Following in the footsteps of his father and grandfather, Bell worked with students who were deaf. Because they couldn't hear, these students had a hard time learning to speak. Bell tinkered with devices that could help his students learn words without hearing them. One of his inventions made graphs of sound waves. That allowed people who couldn't hear the sounds to see how different sounds looked.

Bell was passionate about helping individuals with hearing difficulties. This focus on the human voice may have been a key influence in his desire to invent the telephone.

Bell established several schools for the deaf. Here he stands (*top right*) with a group of students at his school in Boston.

SPEEDING UP THE COMMUNICATION GAME

While in Boston, Bell began experimenting with ways to improve long-distance communication. People at the time communicated by **telegraph**. This system used electric signals to send one coded message at a time, in the form of clicks, over a long-distance wire. Bell had an idea for a new system in which several telegraph messages could be sent over a single wire at the same time. He found **investors** who were willing to fund his research and was able to make promising progress.

Hermann von Helmholtz (*pictured*) experimented with how humans perceive sound tones. His work made Bell wonder about transmitting human voices.

Bell was inspired by the work of Hermann von Helmholtz, a German scientist who had studied sound tones. Bell also explored emerging breakthroughs in the many uses of electricity. He hoped to invent a wire that could combine these exciting advancements into a new telegraph system.

He even started dreaming about sending the human voice over these wires. But Bell's investors weren't interested in that, so he was forced to put it aside and work on the multiple-message telegraph.

Bell and Watson performed many of their earliest experiments at Boston University.

Soon the young inventor had help. Bell's investors recruited the talented electrician Thomas Watson to his team. The two worked together on Bell's telegraph. Bell was responsible for coming up with new ideas, and Watson was in charge of using those ideas to build the inventions.

With Watson's help, Bell surged ahead in his work on the telegraph. He was focused on creating a harmonic telegraph line, which could **transmit** multiple messages at once.

ASSIST

Bell spent most of his time working on perfecting the multiple-message telegraph. But his investors noticed that he was distracted. He was also determined to develop what would later become the telephone. To keep Bell on task, his investors hired Thomas Watson (*left*). Watson was in charge of keeping Bell's head in the telegraph game.

In Bell's day, the telegraph used a special device (*above*) to send electrical pulses across a wire in a series of long and short coded signals to spell out messages. However, the wire could only allow one set of electrical pulses to be sent and decoded at a time. Bell wanted to be able to send messages back and forth at the same time.

Bell's investors advised him to apply for a **patent** to protect his idea while he set about perfecting it. He applied for a patent for his harmonic telegraph in February 1875. But he still dreamed of a device that would send the sound of a human voice across a wire. If he could find a way to do it, that machine would prove to be a slam-dunk, world-changing invention!

CHAPTER 2
THE CHALLENGER

Bell wasn't the only competitor in the running to invent a device that could transmit speech. An Italian inventor, Antonio Santi Giuseppe Meucci, was working on his own version of the telephone before Bell had even started work on his harmonic telegraph.

As a young man, Meucci worked as a stagehand at the Teatro della Pergola, an opera house in Florence, Italy. In 1834, he invented a device that allowed communication between different parts of the theater. The invention was made up of two cones connected by an empty

Meucci made his first attempts at transmitting speech while he was working at the Teatro della Pergola (*above*).

Speaking tubes, much like Meucci's opera house invention, were used on ships and in houses starting in the early nineteenth century. They alllowed people on different floors to communicate with one another.

pipe. A person could speak into one end, and the voice would carry through the pipe to a listener on the other end. It was clear that the rookie was already thinking like a pro in the communication game.

AN EXCITING DISCOVERY

Meucci moved to Cuba the following year. He worked at several jobs and continued to invent. In 1848, Meucci took a job performing physical therapy. The young inventor improved upon a system that used electric currents to try to treat pain, such as that caused by arthritis.

Meucci (*above*) stumbled upon the possibility of using electricity to send the human voice through a wire. It took his speaking tubes idea to a whole new level.

Meucci's Staten Island home, where he lived in the latter part of the nineteenth century, was eventually turned into a museum to honor the inventor.

One day, while treating a patient with his improved electrical system, Meucci heard a voice coming from a copper wire running between two rooms. The voice belonged to a person in the next room. Meucci was intrigued. He immediately began experiments to replicate and perfect this new method of voice communication.

A BIG BREAK

In 1850, Meucci and his wife, Esterre, moved to Staten Island, New York. There, he opened a candle factory and

HE DID WHAT?

Meucci left his candle factory (*above*) in the hands of the factory managers. They did not handle his money well.

While Meucci focused on perfecting the telephone, he neglected his businesses and made several bad investments. When it was time to file a patent for his telephone, Meucci couldn't pay the $250 fee. He was forced to file a much cheaper patent caveat, which did not protect his invention. If Meucci had done well in business, he might have gotten credit for inventing the telephone.

continued to work on his inventions. Meucci soon set to work even harder when, in 1855, his wife's arthritis partially **paralyzed** her. He created a **prototype** telephone that would allow them to communicate between his basement laboratory and her second-floor bedroom. He continued to experiment and made more than thirty versions of his prototype before he finally filed a patent caveat in 1871.

Although his idea worked, Meucci continued to struggle financially and was not even able to afford the $10 patent caveat renewal fee after 1873. He would need more funding if he was ever going to bring his sound telegraph to the public.

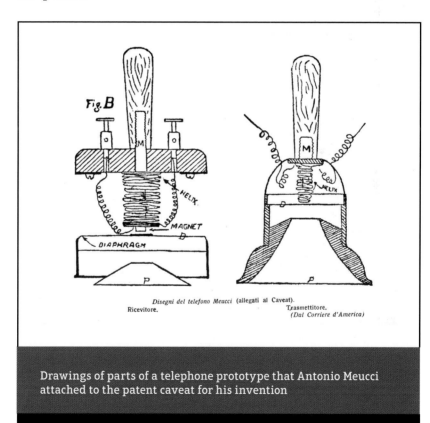

Disegni del telefono Meucci (allegati al Caveat).
Ricevitore.
Trasmettitore.
(Dal Corriere d'America)

Drawings of parts of a telephone prototype that Antonio Meucci attached to the patent caveat for his invention

CHAPTER 3
THE TOURNAMENT OF TELEPHONE TECHNOLOGY

After some success with the harmonic telegraph, Bell and Watson started investigating how their device might be altered to transmit a human voice. Imagining the new possibilities, Bell wrote home to his family, outlining his idea for "an instrument by which the human voice might be telegraphed." He explained that a magnet would

Part of the harmonic telegraph Bell used for some of his earliest telephone experiments in 1876

In 1846, Joseph Henry became the first secretary of the Smithsonian Institute, an organization that included an observatory, a museum, a national library, and a research institute.

start a vibrating current of electricity in the coils of an **electromagnet** to operate the device.

Bell also told the secretary of the Smithsonian Institute, physicist Joseph Henry, about his idea for the telephone. Henry was impressed and encouraged Bell to continue with his telephone experiments. But the pressure to complete his harmonic telegraph meant Bell could not focus all his attention on this exciting new invention.

TRAGEDY AND TRIUMPH

Meanwhile, Meucci was struggling. As Meucci had set off to find financial support to further develop his telephone, tragedy struck. He was riding on a ferry boat when it exploded, leaving him with severe burns. To help pay the medical bills, his wife sold all of his prototypes to a secondhand shop. By the time Meucci was released from the hospital, all of his telephone models had been resold, leaving him with no information on their new owners.

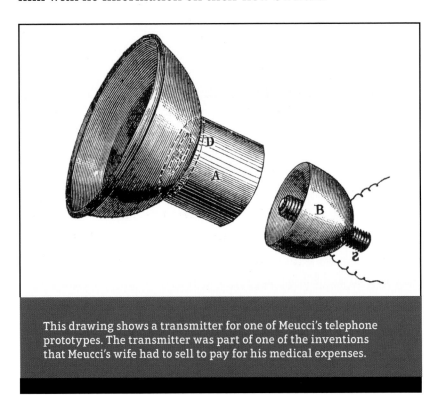

This drawing shows a transmitter for one of Meucci's telephone prototypes. The transmitter was part of one of the inventions that Meucci's wife had to sell to pay for his medical expenses.

Bell (*left*) and Watson (*right*) worked together on the harmonic telegraph and the telephone.

It was a hard blow for Meucci, but the young inventor was determined. He made a new prototype and tried to get a meeting with the Western Union Telegraph Company to pitch his idea. He knew that with the right kind of financial support, he could be back in the game in no time. But he struggled to get a meeting with Western Union. Meanwhile, Bell and Watson were catching up!

After scraping something together, Bell was awarded a patent for his "speaking telegraph" on March 7, 1876. His investors soon realized the potential of this new idea and gave him permission to switch his focus to the telephone full-time.

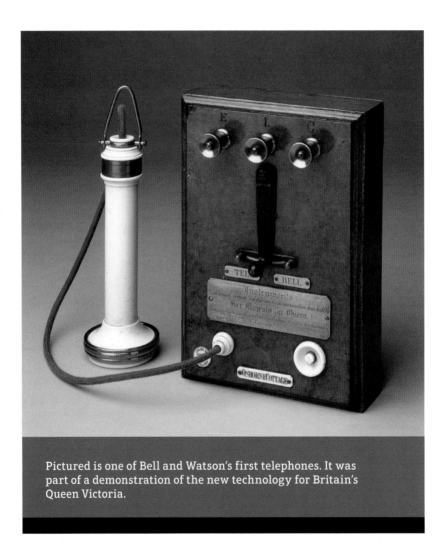

Pictured is one of Bell and Watson's first telephones. It was part of a demonstration of the new technology for Britain's Queen Victoria.

Bell and Watson got to work immediately. Bell thought a different battery would strengthen the electric current that carried the sound through the wire. The two men also tweaked their device to help the wire pick up the signal better. On March 10, they set up a **receiver** on the dresser in Bell's bedroom and ran a wire to the next room. Bell spoke through the receiver. "Mr. Watson, come here, I want to see you." It was a success!

HE DID WHAT?

After the telephone's creation, many people were excited to have one installed in their home or place of business. Communication across long distances became simple, making everyday life much easier. Even after inventing the telephone in his laboratory (*left*), Bell refused to have one in his study. He feared it would distract him from his scientific work.

CHAPTER 4
POSTGAME

Following his first successful telephone call, Bell spent the next year traveling in Europe, where he spent some time demonstrating his invention. Bell was experiencing the success of his world-changing invention. But the battle wasn't over yet. In 1886, Meucci sued Bell for patent **infringement**.

Bell demonstrates his telephone.

This vintage illustration of an amazed woman listening to her first telephone call depicts the excited reaction from the public to the new invention.

During the legal battle, Meucci was able to give very specific details about the device he had invented. But Bell had gained the financial support of Western Union, and Meucci's patent caveat did not describe an electric telephone. Meucci was fighting a losing battle.

The court case between Meucci and Bell continued until 1889, when Meucci died. The case was dropped, and many forgot that another player had competed in the race to invent the telephone.

THE FINAL CALL

Both Bell and Meucci made amazing advancements in the field of long-distance communication. However, Meucci's lack of financial support meant he received very little recognition for his invention and was never able to perfect his prototypes or bring his invention to the public. Meanwhile, Bell went on to organize the Bell Telephone Company in 1877. Within ten years, over 150,000 people in the United States got telephones. Bell became the telephone's MVP.

In this image of the Bell Telephone office at Hamburg, New York, in the early twentieth century, two women operate a switchboard.

THE WINNER!

BELL

INVENTOR MATCHUP

BELL

- **INSPIRATION:** Communication for deaf students
- **TEAM OR SOLO:** Team
- **BUSINESSES:** Successful Bell Telephone Company
- **TOTAL PATENTS FILED (LIFETIME):** 30

MEUCCI

- **INSPIRATION:** Communication with his ill wife
- **TEAM OR SOLO:** Solo
- **BUSINESSES:** Failed candle factory
- **TOTAL PATENTS FILED (LIFETIME):** 14

TIMELINE

1834
Antoni Santi Giuseppe Meucci invents a device for communicating across distances at the Teatro della Pergola, an opera house in Florence, Italy.

1855
Meucci designs his first working telephone prototype. He uses it in his home to communicate with his disabled wife.

1871
Alexander Graham Bell moves to Boston, Massachusetts, and becomes a speech teacher. Meucci files a patent caveat for his telephone.

FEBRUARY 1876
Bell files a patent for his telephone.

MARCH 10, 1876
Bell and Watson successfully make their first telephone call between two rooms in Bell's laboratory.

JULY 9, 1877
Bell founds Bell Telephone Company.

OCTOBER 18, 1889
The patent infringement court case between Meucci and Bell is dropped after Meucci dies.

SOURCE NOTES

18 Edwin S. Grosvenor and Morgan Wesson, *Alexander Graham Bell: The Life and Times of the Man Who Invented the Telephone* (New York: Harry N. Abrams, 1997), 51.

23 Ibid., 67.

GLOSSARY

electromagnet: magnetic material surrounded by a coil of wire through which an electric current is passed

infringement: failure to uphold the law, usually by violating someone's rights

investors: people who give or lend money to an inventor or company with the understanding that they will get a share of any profits

paralyzed: to have completely or partially lost function especially when involving motion or feeling in a part of the body

patent: a legal document that gives an inventor the sole right to make or sell an invention

patent caveat: a document describing an invention and announcing the intention of taking out a patent at a later date

prototype: the first model of an invention, which is later copied to make more

receiver: the part of a telephone in which electrical signals are converted into sound

telegraph: a device for sending messages over long distances using a code of electrical signals sent by wire or radio

transmit: to send a signal by radio waves or over a wire

FURTHER INFORMATION

Alexander Graham Bell
http://www.history.com/topics/inventions/alexander
-graham-bell

Antonio Meucci
http://www.famousinventors.org/antonio-meucci

Einhorn, Kama. *The 4-1-1 on Phones!* New York: Simon
Spotlight, 2015.

Everyday Mysteries: Who Is Credited as Inventing the
Telephone?
https://www.loc.gov/rr/scitech/mysteries/telephone.html

Jackson, Tom. *Telephones and Cell Phones.* Tucson, AZ: Brown
Bear, 2015.

Lin, Yoming S. *Alexander Graham Bell and the Telephone.* New
York: PowerKids, 2012.

Schuman, Michael. *Alexander Graham Bell: Scientist and
Inventor.* Berkeley Heights, NJ: Enslow, 2015.

Who Made America? Alexander Graham Bell
http://www.pbs.org/wgbh/theymadeamerica/whomade
/bell_hi.html

INDEX

PHOTO ACKNOWLEDGMENTS

The images in this book are used with the permission of: iStock.com/gpointstudio, p. 4; iStock.com/vitranc, p. 5 (girl on the phone); iStock.com/Leszek Kobusinski, p. 5 (iPhone); National Geographic Stock: Vintage Collection/The Granger Collection, New York, p. 6; Time Life Pictures/The LIFE Picture Collection/Getty Images, p. 7; iStock.com/ZU_09, p. 8; George Brayton/Wikimedia Commons (PD), p. 9; SSPL/Getty Images, pp. 10, 22; De Agostini/Getty Images, pp. 11, 16; Manuelarosi/Wikimedia Commons (CC BY-SA 3.0), p. 12; Print Collector/Hulton Archive/Getty Images, pp. 13, 24; Leemage/Corbis Historical/Getty Images, p. 14; Randy Duchaine/Alamy Stock Photo, p. 15; Mondadori Portfolio/Getty Images, pp. 17, 20; © Museums Victoria / CC BY 4.0, p. 18; Library of Congress (LC-DIG-cwpbh-00489), p. 19; Bettmann/Getty Images, p. 21; Time Life Pictures/The LIFE Picture Collection/Getty Images, p. 23; GraphicaArtis/Hulton Archive/Getty Images, p. 25; Library of Congress (LC-USZ62-11823), p. 26; Universal History Archive/UIG/Getty Images, pp. 27, 28 (Bell headshot); L. Alman/Wikimedia Commons (CC BY 4.0), p. 28 (Meucci headshot); iStock.com/lushik, p. 28 (boxing glove bullets). Design elements: iStock.com/ivanastar; iStock.com/Allevinatis; iStock.com/subtropica.

Front cover: iStock.com/ivanastar (background); iStock.com/Allevinatis (boxer); iStock.com/winterling (telephone); Universal History Archive/UIG/Getty Images (Alexander Graham Bell); L. Alman/Wikimedia Commons (CC BY 4.0) (Antonio Meucci).